D1402882

Celebrate!

Italy

Robyn Hardyman

CHELSEA CLUBHOUSE

An Imprint of Chelsea House Publishers

Chelsea Clubhouse
An imprint of Chelsea House
132 West 31st Street
New York, NY 10001

Library of Congress Cataloging-in-Publication Data

Hardyman, Robyn.
  Celebrate Italy / Robyn Hardyman. — 1st ed.
      p. cm. — (Celebrate)
  Includes bibliographical references and index.
  ISBN 978-1-60413-269-4
  1. Italy—Juvenile literature. 2. Italy—Social life and customs—Juvenile literature. I. Title.
  DG417.H37 2009
  945—dc22
                        2008030559

Chelsea Clubhouse books are available at special discounts when purchased in bulk quantities for businesses, associations, institutions, or sales promotions. Please call our Special Sales Department in New York at (212) 967-8800 or (800) 322-8755.

You can find Chelsea House on the World Wide Web at http://www.chelseahouse.com

Printed and bound in China

10 9 8 7 6 5 4 3 2 1

This book is printed on acid-free paper.

All links and Web addresses were checked and verified to be correct at the time of publication. Because of the dynamic nature of the Web, some addresses and links may have changed since publication and may no longer be valid.

For The Brown Reference Group Ltd.
Project Editor: Sarah Eason
Designer: Paul Myerscough
Picture Researcher: Maria Joannou
Indexer: Claire Throp
Design Manager: David Poole
Managing Editor: Miranda Smith
Editorial Director: Lindsey Lowe

Consultant Editor
Peter Lewis
Writer and Editor for the American Geographical Society, New York

Author
Robyn Hardyman

Picture Credits
Front Cover: Shutterstock: William Casey, Polartern (t), Chlorophylle (b).
Alamy Images: Caro 26r, Dennis Hallinan 22r, The London Art Archive 21t; Corbis: Marco Bucco/EPA 28b, Sandro Vannini 29b; Fotolia: 16t; Getty Images: Shaun Botterill 12-13; Istockphoto: 3c, 5l, 9t, 9b, 11tl, 13c, 18t, 24l, 27c; Science Photo Library: Royal Astronomical Society 9r; Shutterstock: 3t, 3b, 4b, 6c, 8t, 8l, 8r, 10c, 11tr, 11b, 13r, 14t, 14b, 15l, 15r, 16b, 17, 18b, 19t, 19cl, 19bl, 20t, 20b, 21c, 21br, 23tl, 23tr, 23b, 24r, 25r, 26l, 27t, 27b, 28-29, 29r, Wikipedia: 12l

Artworks and maps © The Brown Reference Group Ltd.

Contents

Welcome to Italy

Italy has been a single, united nation for less than 150 years (see page 8). The landscape of Italy varies greatly, from high mountains in the north to sunny beaches in the south. The whole country, however, has a rich cultural history, which makes it one of the most popular destinations in the world for visitors.

The **peninsula** of Italy is divided into twenty regions, and each one has a capital city. For example, Milan is the capital of Lombardy and Naples is the capital of Campania. Each region also has its own local government and a **president**. The whole country is then united under a president and a **prime minister**.

Italy

France

Austria

Switzerland

Slovenia

Italy

Mediterranean Sea

Sicily

Venice
Venice is a city in northern Italy. It is built on 120 tiny islands which are connected by about 400 bridges. Instead of roads, Venice has canals of sea water. People get from place to place in long, narrow boats known as gondolas (**right**).

Italian borders

Italy mostly borders the Mediterranean Sea but its land borders are with France, Switzerland, Austria, and Slovenia.

ITALIAN FACTS

FULL NAME	Italian Republic
CAPITAL CITY	Rome
AREA	116,346 square miles
POPULATION IN 2008	58,147,733
MAIN LANGUAGE	Italian
MAIN RELIGION	Roman Catholic
CURRENCY	Euro

Leaning Tower of Pisa

The Leaning Tower of Pisa is the bell tower of Pisa's cathedral. It is one of the most famous buildings in the world. It began to lean soon after building began in 1173, because its foundations were poorly laid. Between 1990 and 2001 the tower was partly straightened, so today it is stable.

Emblem of Italy

This is the **emblem** of Italy. It appears on the cover of an Italian European passport.

History Highlights

Two thousand years ago, Italy was at the center of a great empire. The Roman Empire at its height, in about 170 C.E., included most of western Europe, the Middle East, and North Africa.

In 410 C.E. **barbarian** tribes invaded the empire and captured Rome. In the following centuries, the buildings and other parts of ancient Roman life fell into ruin. Italy was not a single united country, but a collection of smaller states each centered on a major city. These **city-states** were ruled by powerful families. For several centuries there was fighting between the city-states.

Colosseum

The Colosseum is an ampitheater. It was the biggest building in ancient Rome. Wild animal shows and gladiator fights were held here in front of audiences of up to 50,000 people.

WEB LINKS
To find out more about ancient Rome go to:
www.historyforkids.org/learn/romans

Marco Polo

Marco Polo (1254–1324) was one of the few Europeans to visit China in the Middle Ages. In 1271 he began an extraordinary journey by camel along the **Silk Road**, a long road from China to Iran that linked China to the West. Polo met the Chinese Emperor Kublai Khan (reigned 1260–94) in 1274 and spent time in his court. Polo returned to Italy twenty-four years later, and wrote about his adventures.

The Roman army

The Roman army was the best organized and best trained army in the world. Roman soldiers were not only powerful fighters, they were also skilled engineers. The Roman army built forts, roads, and bridges in countries they conquered, many of which still stand today.

Great builders

The Romans were great **architects** and builders. Their magnificent public buildings included temples, law courts, ampitheaters, bath houses, and even chariot race stadiums.

Italy becomes one country

In the fifteenth century, educated people in Italy rediscovered the art of ancient Greece and Rome in a movement called the **Renaissance** (rebirth). Conflict between the city-states continued, however, and Italy was ruled first by Spain (1559–1713) and then by Austria (1713–96). In the nineteenth century the city-states united, and in 1870 Italy became a single nation, ruled by a king, Victor Emmanuel III. The Pope would not accept **unification** (union). He continued to rule Vatican City, which, as a **principality**, is still independent of the rest of Italy today.

Vatican City

Rome

DID YOU KNOW?
The smallest country in the world is the Vatican City. It is only 108 acres large and is surrounded by a high wall. The city lies within Rome and has its own supermarket, post office, bank, police service, fire brigade, railway station, electricity generating plant, radio, and television center.

Protecting the Pope
The Swiss Guards have been protecting the Pope in the Vatican since 1506. Although their uniforms are decorative, they are highly trained soldiers.

Galileo Galilei

Galileo Galilei (1564–1642) was a scientist, mathematician, and **astronomer**. He was one of the first people to look at space through a telescope. Galileo was convinced that the Earth and planets moved around the Sun at a time when most people thought the opposite was true.

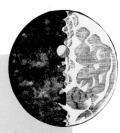

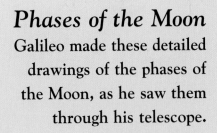

Phases of the Moon
Galileo made these detailed drawings of the phases of the Moon, as he saw them through his telescope.

Italy and the world wars

In World War I, Italy sided with Britain, France, and the United States against Germany and Austria. After the war, however, a **dictator** called Benito Mussolini came to power in Italy. Mussolini formed an alliance with the German leader Adolf Hitler. Italy entered World War II on the side of Germany. After the war, Italians voted to become a **republic**. This stamp from World War II shows Mussolini (right) with Hitler (left).

Fly the Flag

The national flag of Italy has three vertical stripes of green, white, and red. It is known as the tricolore, which means "three colors." The green side of the Italian flag is attached to a flag pole.

Until Italy became one united nation in 1870, each state had its own flag. Between 1848 and 1870, the tricolore was a symbol that united the Italian people in their struggle toward freedom and independence. Between 1870 and 1947, the flag had on it the coat of arms of the ruling royal family, the House of Savoy.

Giuseppe Garibaldi

Giuseppe Garibaldi (1807–82) is an Italian national hero. It was under his leadership that Italian soldiers brought many city-states under control, which helped to create a united Italy.

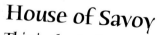

House of Savoy

This is the Italian flag at the time of the House of Savoy. On the state flag the shield had a crown above it.

Vatican City

This is the flag of Vatican City. It features the crossed keys of Saint Peter and the Papal Tiara, or Pope's crown. Saint Peter was the first head of the Catholic Church and the Pope is the head today.

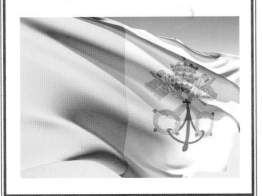

DID YOU KNOW?

The inspiration for the colors and design of the modern Italian flag came from the French flag. Some northern Italian city-states adopted the colors of the French flag during Napoleon's invasion of Italy in 1796. The green, white, and red design of the national Italian flag was later based upon the flags of these northern city-states.

🏳 *Try this!*

Make an Italian pencil holder

- *On a piece of white paper mark out three rectangles 2 inches wide by about 6 inches long. Paint one rectangle green and one red. Leave the third one white.*

- *When the paint has dried, cut out the three rectangles.*

- *Trim a cardboard tube from inside a toilet roll so that it is 6 inches long.*

- *Cut out a circle of card a little bigger than one end of the tube, and make small cuts round its edge. Stick this over one end, folding the cut pieces up around the sides, to form the base of the pot.*

- *Now stick the colored rectangles around the tube. Put green at the top, then white, then red. Trim them to fit exactly around the tube.*

Hymn to Italy

Italy's colorful and dramatic history has meant that the country has had more than one national anthem since unification.

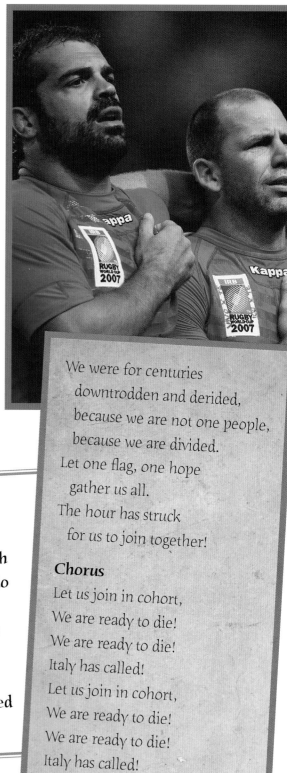

*I*l Canto degli Italiani (*The Song of the Italians*) is the Italian **national anthem** today. It is best known among Italians as *Inno di Mameli* (*Mameli's Hymn*), or *Fratelli d'Italia* (*Brothers of Italy*). The words were written in 1847 by a student from Genoa named Goffredo Mameli. They refer to Italy's struggle for unification and independence.

We were for centuries
downtrodden and derided,
because we are not one people,
because we are divided.
Let one flag, one hope
gather us all.
The hour has struck
for us to join together!

Chorus
Let us join in cohort,
We are ready to die!
We are ready to die!
Italy has called!
Let us join in cohort,
We are ready to die!
We are ready to die!
Italy has called!

Goffredo Mameli

On the right is one verse of the national anthem with its rousing chorus. Goffredo Mameli wrote the words when he was only 20 years old. He was injured defending the Roman Republic against the French in 1849 and died a month later at the age of 22.

Rugby song

The Italian rugby team (left), and fans of the national soccer team (below), proudly sing the national anthem at their international matches.

An earlier anthem

After unification in 1870, Italy chose a song called the *Marcia Reale* (below) as its anthem. This remained the national anthem until Italy became a republic in 1947. Then *The Song of the Italians* was chosen as the new anthem. This choice was only formally accepted in 2005, almost sixty years later.

DID YOU KNOW?

Mameli's Hymn was first written without words. Two months after he composed it, the writer Michele Novaro wrote the words.

WEB LINKS

To hear the Italian national anthem go to: www.national-anthems.net/IT

Regions of Italy

Italy forms a peninsula that faces southeast into the Mediterranean Sea. The islands of Sicily, Sardinia, Elba, and Capri are also part of the country. So too are the separate principalities of Vatican City and San Marino.

I taly has dramatic mountains, grassy plains, and beautiful beaches. In the north, winters are cold and summers are hot. The best agricultural (farming) land is in the north. Most industry is there also. The south is warmer, with a **Mediterranean climate**. Here the land is not as fertile, and there is less industry.

A land of mountains

Italy has three mountain ranges: the Alps in the northwest, the Dolomites in the northeast, and the Apennines, which extend for 860 miles down the center of the country.

Wildlife
The rare ibex lives in the Gran Paradiso national park in northwest Italy.

Coastal beauty

The Amalfi Coast is a stretch of coastline on the west coast of Italy. Renowned for its rugged terrain, scenic beauty, picturesque towns and diversity, the Amalfi Coast is a World Heritage Site.

Sicily

The beautiful island of Sicily in the Mediterranean Sea is part of Italy. Sicily has been occupied by many peoples over the centuries, so it has many historic sites. At Syracuse, an ancient Greek theater (below) stands to this day, and plays are still performed there.

Volcanoes

Sicily's Mount Etna is one of the world's most active volcanoes. Its lava flows destroy local villages every few years. Mount Vesuvius, near Naples, erupts less often, but can be devastating. Its eruption of 79 C.E. buried the towns of Pompeii (above) and Herculaneum.

What's Cooking?

Italian pasta and pizza are popular throughout the world. Both of these are typical Italian dishes, but each region of Italy has its own specialties.

In central Italy, olive oil and beef are specialities of Tuscany, while Parmesan cheese and Parma ham are made in Emilia–Romagna in the north. The south has superb fruit, herbs, and seafood, and many dishes use tomatoes. Many of Italy's finest cheeses are made in the north.

Wine
Italy is the world's biggest producer of wine. Italian wines include Chianti, a red wine from Tuscany, and Frascati, a white wine from Lazio, near Rome.

DID YOU KNOW?

The Italians serve their coffee in many different ways. A cappuccino is coffee mixed with hot milk and topped with foamy milk. A caffelatte is strong coffee mixed with hot milk. An espresso is a very small and strong coffee, which is served in a tiny cup.

Spaghetti sauce

The Bolognese sauce on this spaghetti was first created in the city of Bologna.

What's on the menu?

A full Italian meal has the following courses:

antipasto (starter)
sliced salami

il primo (first course)
tagliatelle (ribbon pasta) with butter and sage

il secondo (main course)
vitello (veal) with lemon sauce and green beans

dolce (dessert)
tiramisu (creamy pudding)
or gelati (ice cream)
formaggio (cheese)
espresso (strong, small coffee)

Try this!

Let's make fusilli al tonno (tuna pasta)

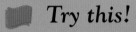

Ingredients:
14 oz fusilli (spiral pasta)
2 fl oz olive oil
1 small onion, chopped
1 clove of garlic, crushed
5 oz canned tuna
14-oz can chopped tomatoes
salt and pepper

Put the olive oil, crushed garlic, and chopped onion in a frying pan. Fry over low heat until the onion is golden brown. Add the chopped tomatoes, salt, and pepper. Cook gently for about 5 minutes, and then add the tuna. Cook gently for a further 10 minutes. While the sauce is cooking, bring to a boil a saucepan full of water. When it is bubbling, ask an adult to add the fusilli pasta. Boil for 10 minutes. Ask an adult to drain the pasta and return it to the saucepan. Add the sauce to the pasta and stir well. Serve onto warmed plates.

How Do I Say...?

For most people in Italy their first language is the dialect of their local region. Most people also speak Italian.

Modern Italian comes from Latin, the language of the ancient Romans, and then from the **dialect** of Tuscany, a region in northern Italy. The Tuscan dialect became the most widely used because the three great writers of the Middle Ages—Dante, Boccaccio, and Petrarch—wrote in the Tuscan dialect.

Words and phrases

English	Italian	How to say it
hello	buon giorno	bwon jaw-no
goodbye	arrivederci	aree-ved-air-chee
please	per favore	pair fav-oray
thank you	grazie	grat-zee-ay
yes	si	see
no	no	noh
Excuse me	Mi scusi	me skoo-zee
How are you?	Come sta?	kom-ay stah
My name is ...	Mi chiama ...	me kee-ama

Some slang expressions

È di luna buona. "He/she is in a good mood."

Parlare fuori dai denti. "To speak outside of one's teeth." This means to say what is on your mind.

Modern Italian

Ancient Romans spoke a language called Latin. The words carved into this ancient stone tablet are in Latin. Modern day Italian has grown out of the Latin language and many Italian words are very similar to Latin ones.

Italian sayings

Ho una fame da lupi.
"I'm hungry like the wolf."

Chi trova un amico trova un tesoro.
"Who finds a friend finds a treasure."

DID YOU KNOW?
The informal word *ciao* can be used to mean either "hello" or "goodbye."

WEB LINKS
To hear more contemporary Italian expressions go to:
www.bbc.co.uk/languages/italian/cool/

Stories and Legends

There are hundreds of folktales in Italian literature. They take readers into a world of adventurers, tricksters, kings, maidens, peasants, and saints. The children's stories of Cinderella and Pinocchio were originally Italian folktales.

In one Italian story, Parrot, a handsome prince, must save the woman he loves from being taken away by an evil king. The prince turns himself into a parrot and holds the woman's attention by telling her an enchanting tale until she is safe from danger.

Romulus and Remus

According to legend, the city of Rome was founded in 753 B.C.E. by Romulus and Remus. These twin boys were the sons of the god Mars. They were abandoned, but found and raised by a wolf. The city's name comes from Romulus.

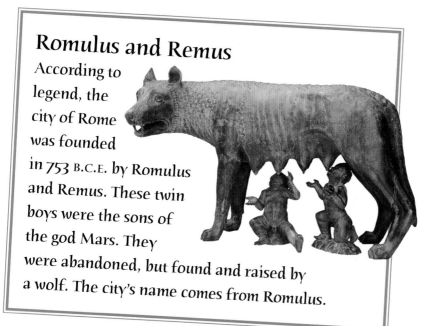

DID YOU KNOW?
In Rome, in a wall of the church called Santa Maria in Cosmedin, there is an ancient marble sculpture called *La Bocca della Verità* ("the mouth of truth"). In the Middle Ages people used this statue as a lie detector by speaking with their hand inside the mouth of the sculpture. They believed that if they told a lie, the sculpture would bite off their hand!

Dante Alighieri

Dante Alighieri (1265–1321) is Italy's most famous poet. His greatest work was *The Divine Comedy*, a very long poem that tells of his travels through the three realms of the dead: Hell, Purgatory, and Paradise. Dante is sometimes called the "the Father of the Italian language."

Pinocchio

This famous story is about a wooden boy puppet that comes to life. It was written by an Italian, Carlo Collodi, and published in 1883. Pinocchio's nose grows longer every time he tells a lie and he learns about life through his adventures.

Tarantula dance

In medieval legend, the women of the town of Taranto were bitten by tarantulas (spiders). The bites sent the women into a trance, from which they could only be cured by frenzied dancing! The *tarantella* dance is today performed by Italians on special occasions.

WEB LINKS

Find out more about the story of Romulus and Remus at:
www.historyonthenet.com/Romans/legend_of_rome.htm

Art and Culture

Italy has a magnificent cultural history. The Italian Renaissance produced some of the greatest artists ever seen. Since then, painters, architects, musicians, and artists of many kinds have lived and worked in the country.

Leonardo da Vinci (1452–1519) and Michelangelo Buonarroti (1475–1564) were two of the greatest artists of the Italian Renaissance. They both trained in Florence, and were great rivals. Michelangelo painted with a realistic style and power that had not been seen before. Leonardo was interested in revealing people's personalities in his paintings. He was a brilliant inventor and scientist, too.

Siena Town Hall
The magnificent town hall in Siena is part of the finest medieval square in Italy.

Oldest festival
Florence's "Maggio Musicale" is one of Italy's oldest music festivals. It features opera, orchestras, and ballet.

Movies

The Cinecittà Studios in Rome are the largest in Europe. Many classic movies were made there in the 1950s and 1960s, including *Ben Hur* (1959). Zeffirelli's *Romeo and Juliet* was also made there in 1968.

A mysterious smile

The Mona Lisa, by Leonardo da Vinci, is one of the most famous paintings in the world. It is a portrait of Lisa del Giocondo, the wife of a wealthy sixteenth century Italian merchant. The painting of Lisa, with her mysterious smile, has become one of the most talked about works of art in history.

Opera

Opera is a combination of classical music, singing, and drama. It began in Italy in the sixteenth century. Famous Italian operas include *Rigoletto* by Verdi and *Tosca* by Puccini.

Statue of David

Michelangelo's Statue of David is the most famous stone sculpture in the history of art. It portrays the Biblical King David as a youth about to battle with the giant Goliath. The statue is 17 feet high.

Fashion

Italians love to look smart and fashionable. Italian fashion designers such as Armani, Gucci, Prada, and Versace are famous all over the world. The northern city of Milan is one of the fashion capitals of the world.

Make Your Own Pizza Solitaire

Try making this solitaire board that looks like a pizza with olives! You play by jumping any counter over its neighbor so that you can remove that counter. The aim is to end up with just one counter left, in the center of the board. Remember—the pizza is a game and is not meant to be eaten!

1 Preheat the oven to 230 °F. Mix the flour, salt, oil, and water in a bowl.

2 Knead the mixture with your hands until it is no longer sticky. Sprinkle a surface with flour and use a rolling pin to roll out the dough. Use a large plate to mark a circle in the dough and cut it out.

3 Line a baking tray with foil and lay the dough inside. Cut out a circle of white paper the same size as the pizza. Draw a circle ½ inch in from the edge of the paper, and a pattern of dots.

4 Lay the paper over the pizza and use the toothpick to prick through the dots and along the circle. Cut a few mushroom and fish shapes from the leftover dough and press them onto the pizza.

DID YOU KNOW?
Italians eat many
different things.
A few of the
unusual items you
might be served in an Italian restaurant
are snails, horse, donkey, goat, wild boar,
peacock, hedgehogs, guinea pigs, sea
urchins, sea snails, octopus and squid!

Ancient pizza

A preserved
flat flour
cake was
found in
the volcanic
ashes of
Pompeii, the town
destroyed by Vesuvius in 79 C.E.
The cake is typical of the food eaten
in Pompeii in Roman times, and is
believed to be the world's oldest pizza.

5 Remove the paper and use the saucer
to make a groove along the inner
circle. Press a small marble into the
toothpick holes to make dents.

6 Roll 32 marble-sized counters out of
the dough, so they fit in the dents on
the pizza. Put them on a separate lined
baking tray. Ask an adult to bake the
board and counters in the oven for 30
minutes. Allow them to cool.

7 Roll the counters in a saucer of watery
black paint so they look like olives.
Paint the pizza, mushrooms, and fish
using poster paints. Add a layer of varnish
when the paints are dry. Have fun!

Sports and Leisure

Italians work hard, but they also enjoy their free time. They like to relax with family and friends over a meal, to travel, and to play sports. Soccer, rugby, cycling, swimming, and skiing are all popular sports in Italy.

Soccer is Italy's favorite sport. Most cities have their own teams, which play in tournaments. Their national soccer team is one of the best in the world. It has won the World Cup four times: in 1934, 1938, 1982, and 2006. Many Italians like to play soccer, too.

Giro d'Italia

The Giro d'Italia is a world famous long-distance bicycle race, held in Italy in May. The route of the 2008 race was over more than 2,100 miles.

WEB LINKS ▼▼▼▼▼▼▼▼▼▼▼▼

The official website of the Giro d'Italia is: www.gazzetta.it/Speciali/Giroditalia

Water sports

Italy has a lot of coastline. The windswept coast of Sardinia is popular for fishing and water sports.

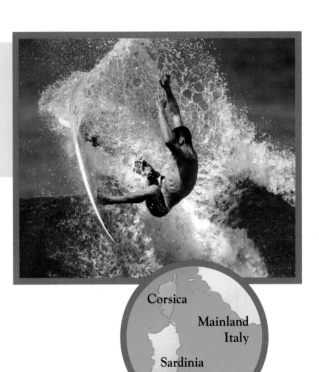

Fabio Cannavaro

The Italian Fabio Cannavaro (born in Naples in 1973) is a World Cup-winning soccer player. He was made captain of Italy's national soccer team in 2002. At club level he plays for Real Madrid. Cannavaro was voted Fifa World Player of the Year in 2006.

Corsica

Mainland Italy

Sardinia

Family

For many Italians their family is an important part of their life. Traditionally, several generations of a family live very near to each other, sometimes in the same house. This is becoming less common today, but Italians still like to spend their free time with family members. It is often an occasion for a large meal and a party.

San Siro

San Siro is the home stadium for two of Milan's soccer teams: A.C. Milan and F.C. Internazionale. It is considered to have one of the best atmospheres of any stadia in the world.

Festivals and Holidays

There are thousands of festivals in Italy each year. These can be important national or religious festivals, or small local celebrations.

Most Italians are Roman Catholic. As well as the major religious holidays, such as Christmas and Easter, Italian cities celebrate a local feast day for their patron saint. The festival for Rome's patron saint is on June 29th, and Milan's is on December 7th.

The Palio

Every summer the city of Siena holds the Palio, an exciting horse race that takes place in July and then again in August. The race dates back to 1310. In a thrilling competition, bareback riders, representing each district of the city, race at top speed three times around the main square. A banner, called the Palio, is presented to the winner. It is decorated with an image of the Virgin Mary.

DID YOU KNOW?
The Palio is over in 90 seconds, but a parade, and a display of flag-waving and flag-throwing takes place before it.

Carnival

Carnevale (meaning "carnival") is held each year in February. People wear bright costumes and enjoy parades and masked balls. The tradition dates from the fourteenth century. Venice is especially famous for its carnival masks.

Food and wine festivals

Rural areas hold local festivals all year round. These are often linked to a particular seasonal food, such as mushrooms or olive oil, or are a celebration of the wine harvest. The people of the village gather for dinner at long tables in the street. After eating, they listen to music and dance.

Republic Day

June 2nd is Republic Day in Italy. This public holiday commemorates the day when Italy became a republic.

Calabrian festival

Every September, Italians travel to a holy site in Calabria, Italy, called the Sanctuary of Saint Maria de Polsi. A festival takes place in celebration of the many miracles believed to have occurred there.

Glossary

ampitheater oval or circular building with tiers of seats around an arena

architects people who design buildings

astronomer person who studies the stars, planets, and space

barbarian person considered to be uneducated and primitive

city-states independent regions much like a country but smaller, consisting of a city and the surrounding territory

climate the average weather conditions over a long period of time

dialect language spoken by people in one region of a country

dictator person who rules a country in a harsh, overbearing way, not allowing anyone to disagree with them

emblem symbol that represents a country

foundations lowest part of a building that helps to support that building

gladiator in ancient Rome, a prisoner, criminal, or slave trained to fight to the death against animals or another gladiator in a public show

gondolas long, narrow boats that are pushed along with a long pole; *gondolas* are used to travel along the canals of Venice

medieval describes the Middle Ages; this period of history was from about 400 to 1450

Mediterranean part of an area of Europe that is found around the Mediterranean Sea, includes countries such as Italy, France, Greece, and Spain

national anthem official song of a country

opera play in which the words are sung to music instead of spoken

peninsula piece of land that is surrounded by water on three sides

president person who runs a country, voted for by its people

prime minister person elected by the people to run a country

principality country ruled by a prince

Renaissance rebirth; a revival of the art and ideas of ancient Greece and Rome that began in Italy in the late fourteenth century

republic a state in which the head of government is not a monarch; republics usually have elected presidents

Silk Road route along which merchants from China took silk to Europe

unification union; joining together of two states

Find Out More

Books

Anderson, Robert. *National Geographic Countries of the World: Italy.* National Geographic Children's Books, 2006

Behnke, Alison. *Italy in Pictures (Visual Geography Series).* Lerner Publications, 2002

Claybourne, Anna. *Time Travel Guides: The Renaissance.* Raintree, 2007

Cooper, Sharon. *Italy ABCs: A Book About the People and Places of Italy.* Picture Window Books, 2003

Fontes, Justine, and Ron Fontes. *Italy (A to Z).* Children's Press, 2003

Goulding, Sylvia. *Festive Foods: Italy.* Chelsea Clubhouse, 2008

Petersen, Christine, and David Petersen. *Italy (True Books).* Children's Press, 2002

Sheen, Barbara. *A Taste of Culture: Foods of Italy.* KidHaven Press, 2005

Web sites

http://kids.yahoo.com/reference/world-factbook/country/it--italy
An excellent Web site that contains many facts about Italy and its people.

www.italianfoodforever.com
You will find lots of delicious recipes for Italian food here.

www.italiantourism.com
You can explore Italy by region at the official site of the Italian tourist board.

www.italyguides.it/us/roma/rome_italy_travel.htm
This site has virtual tours of twelve cities in Italy, including Rome, Venice, Naples, Siena, Florence, and Palermo.

www.pocanticohill.org/italy/italy.htm
Read about Italian life, look at pictures, and play games at this site created by a school in New York.

www.vatican.va
Meet the Pope at official Web site of the world's smallest country, Vatican City.

Index